Do You Have a Ball?

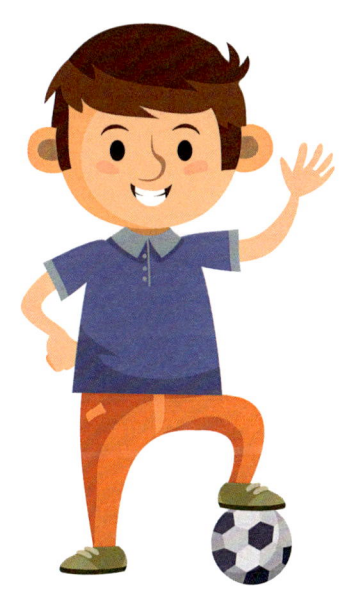

Seed Learning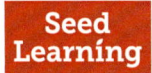

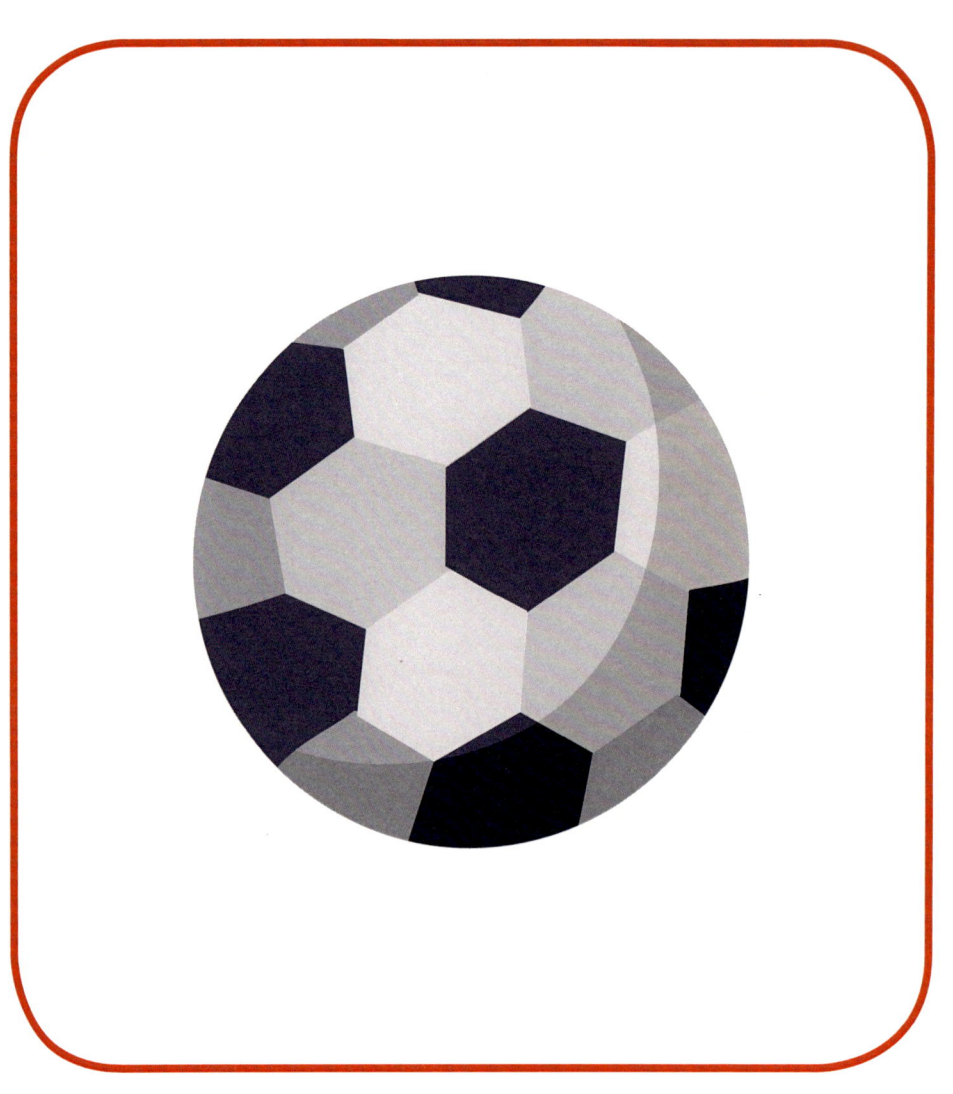

ball

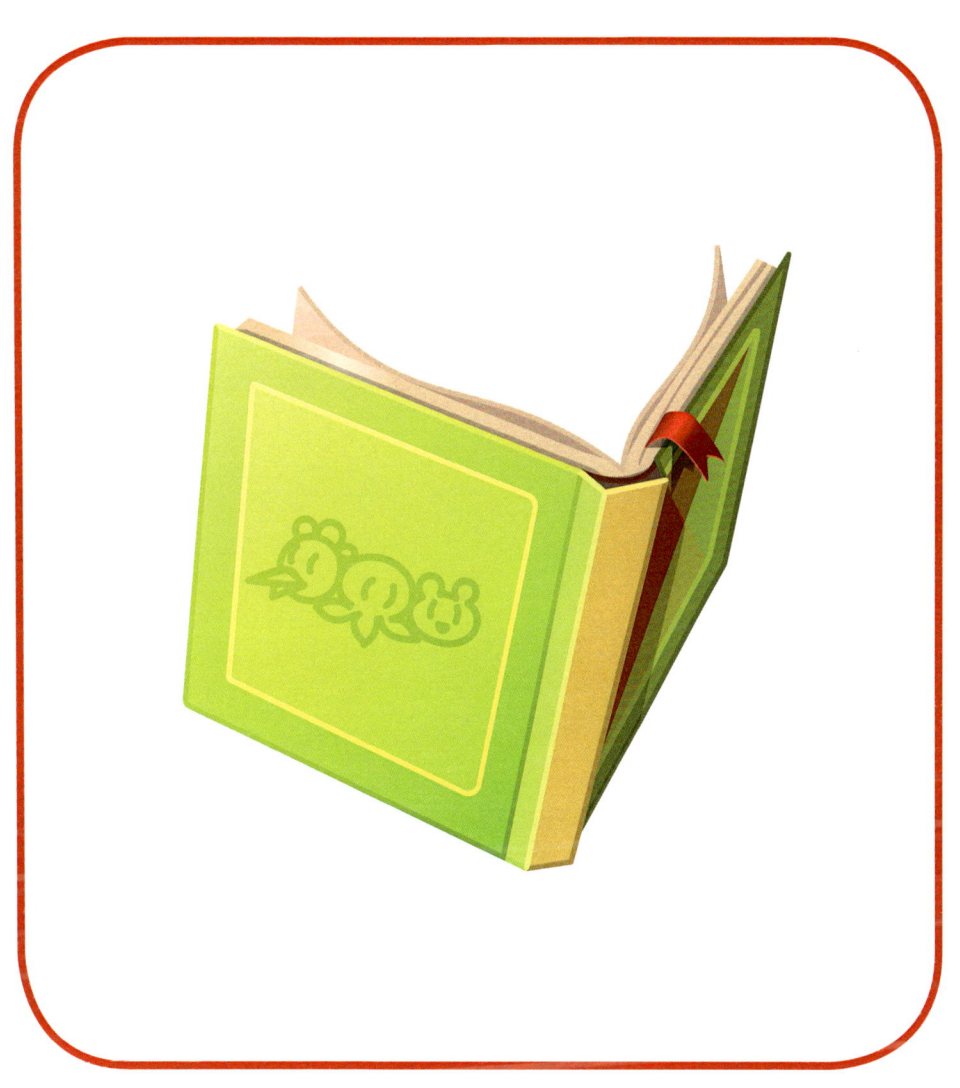

book

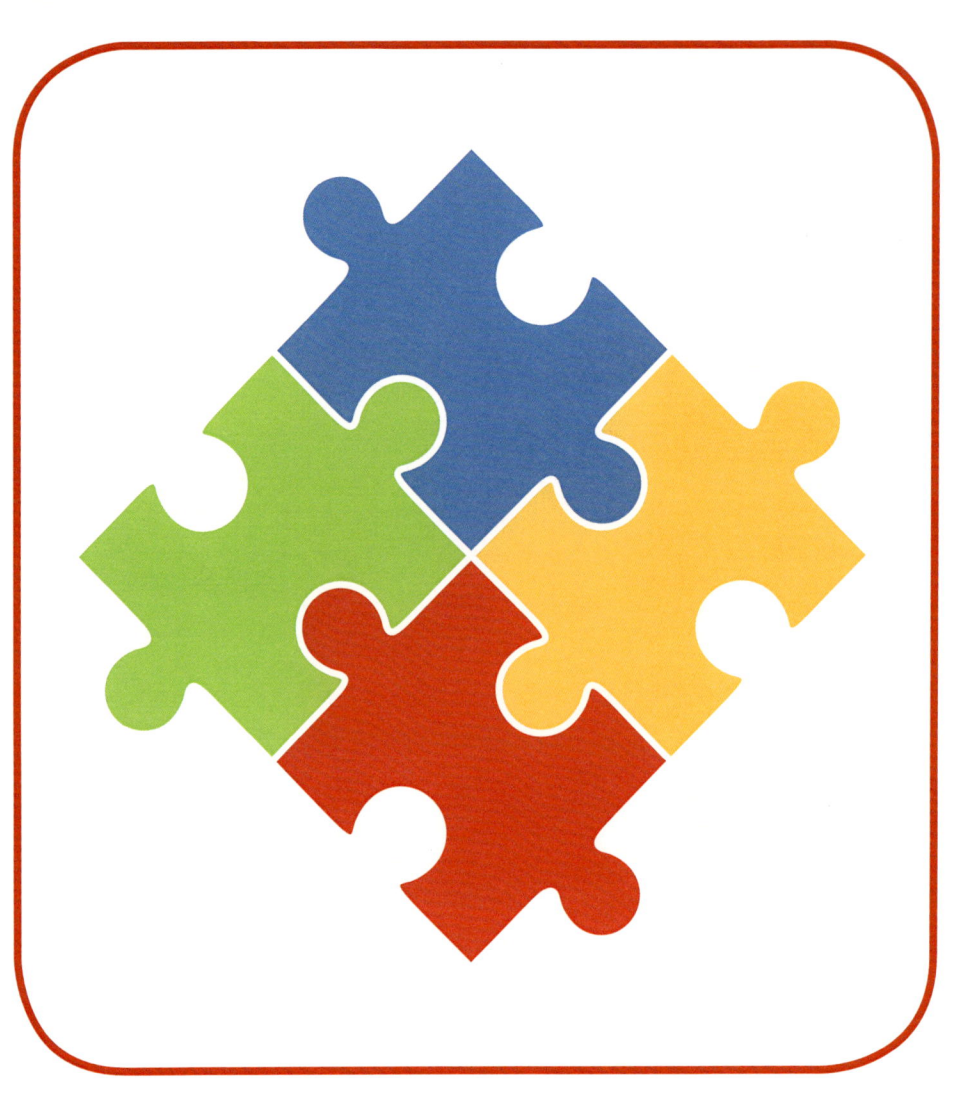

puzzle

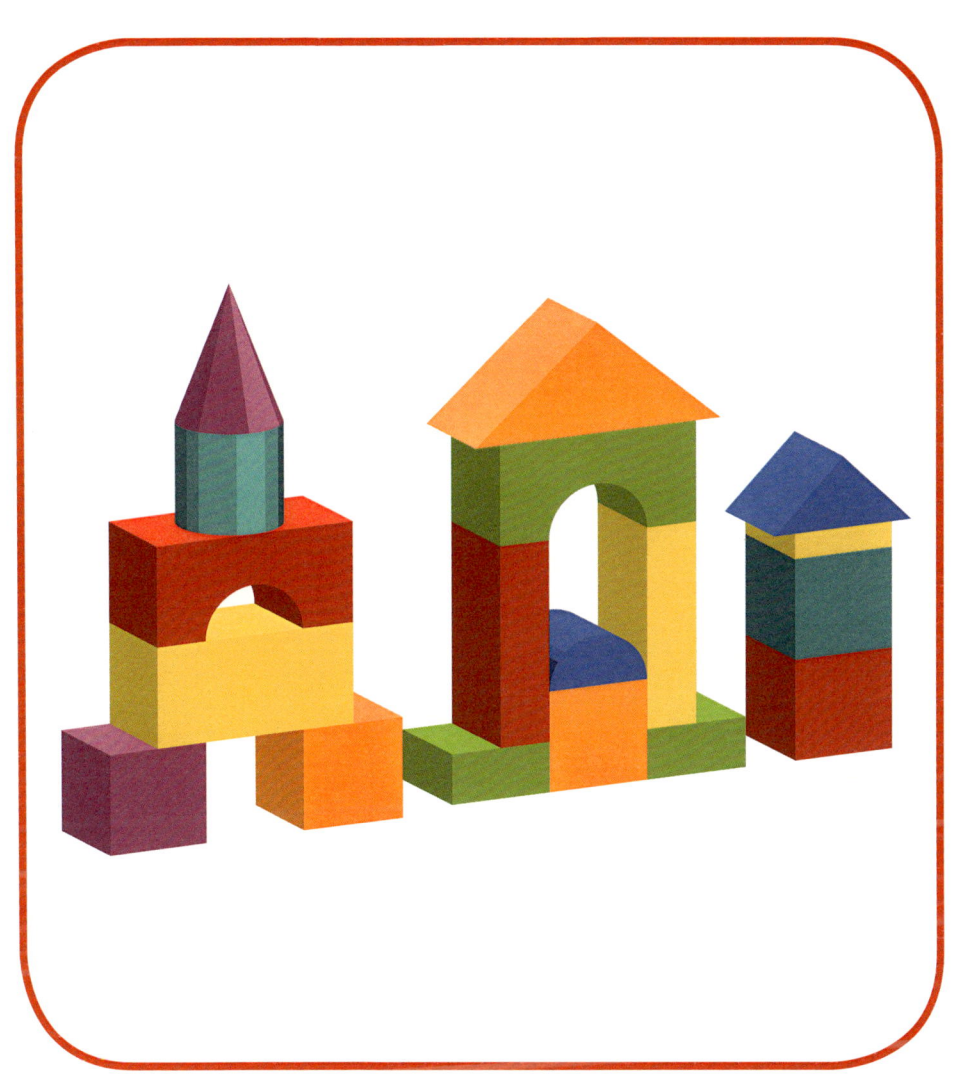

blocks

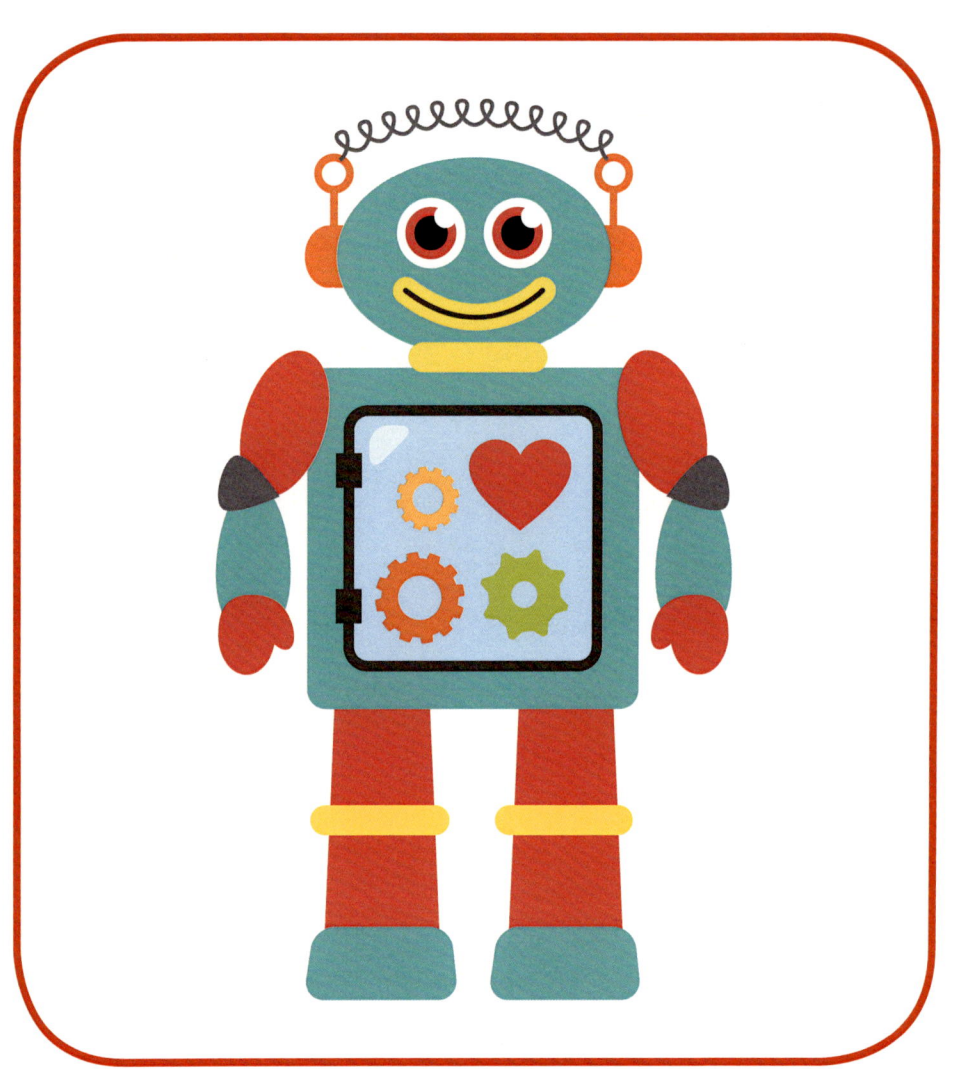

robot

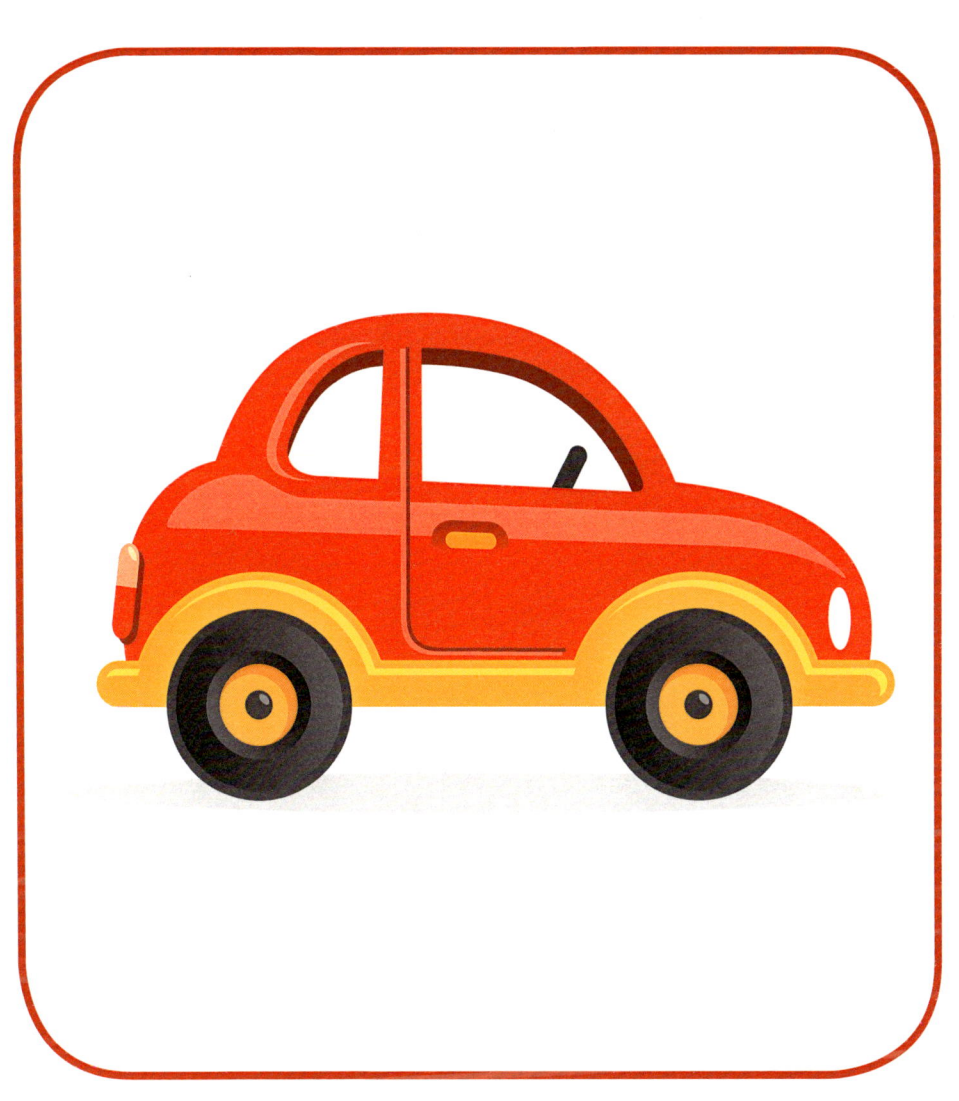

car

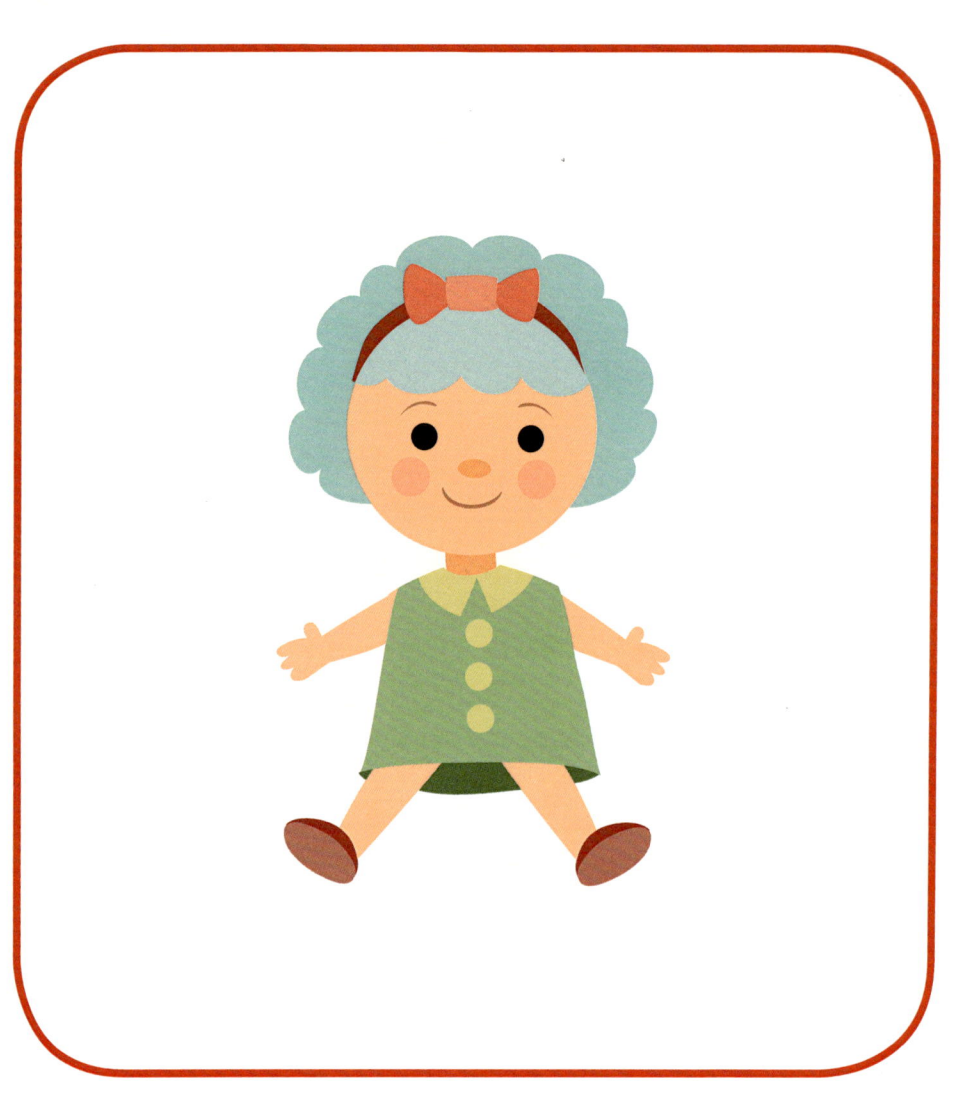

doll

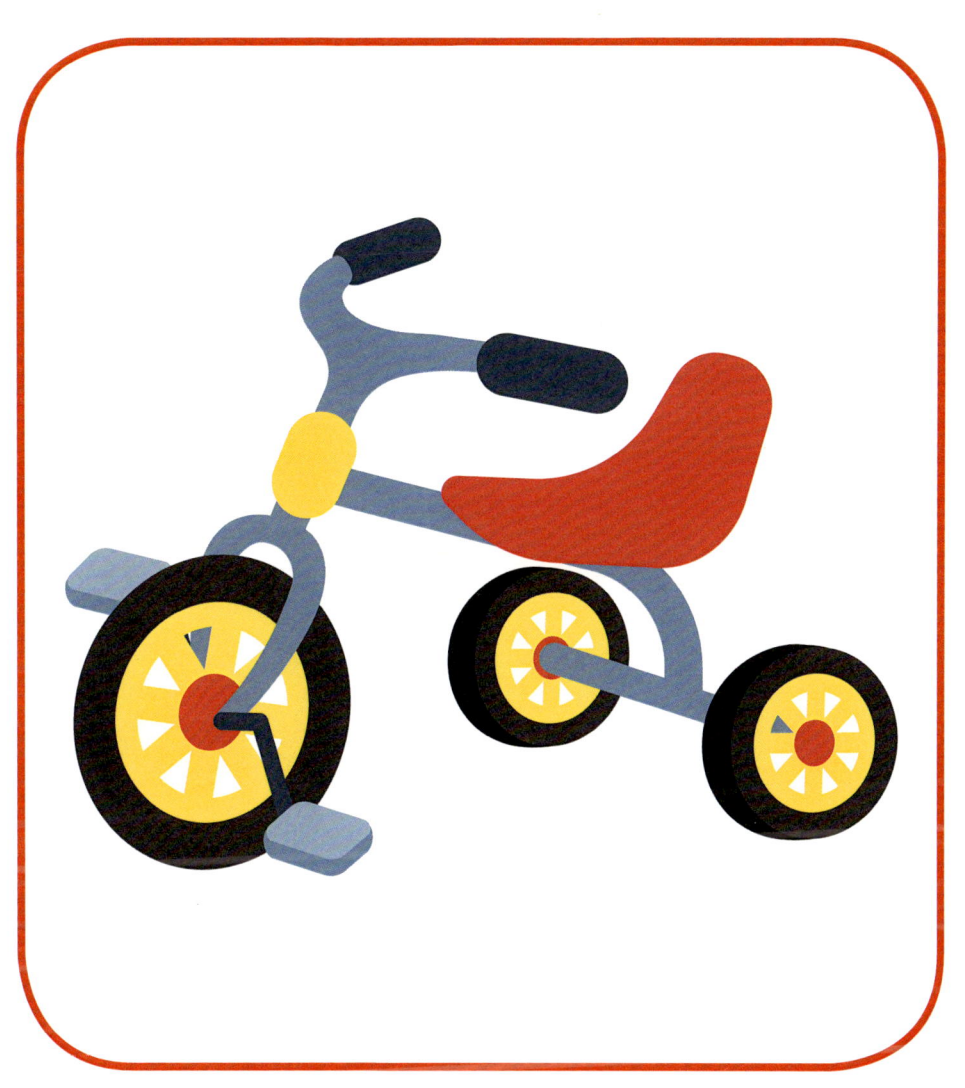

tricycle

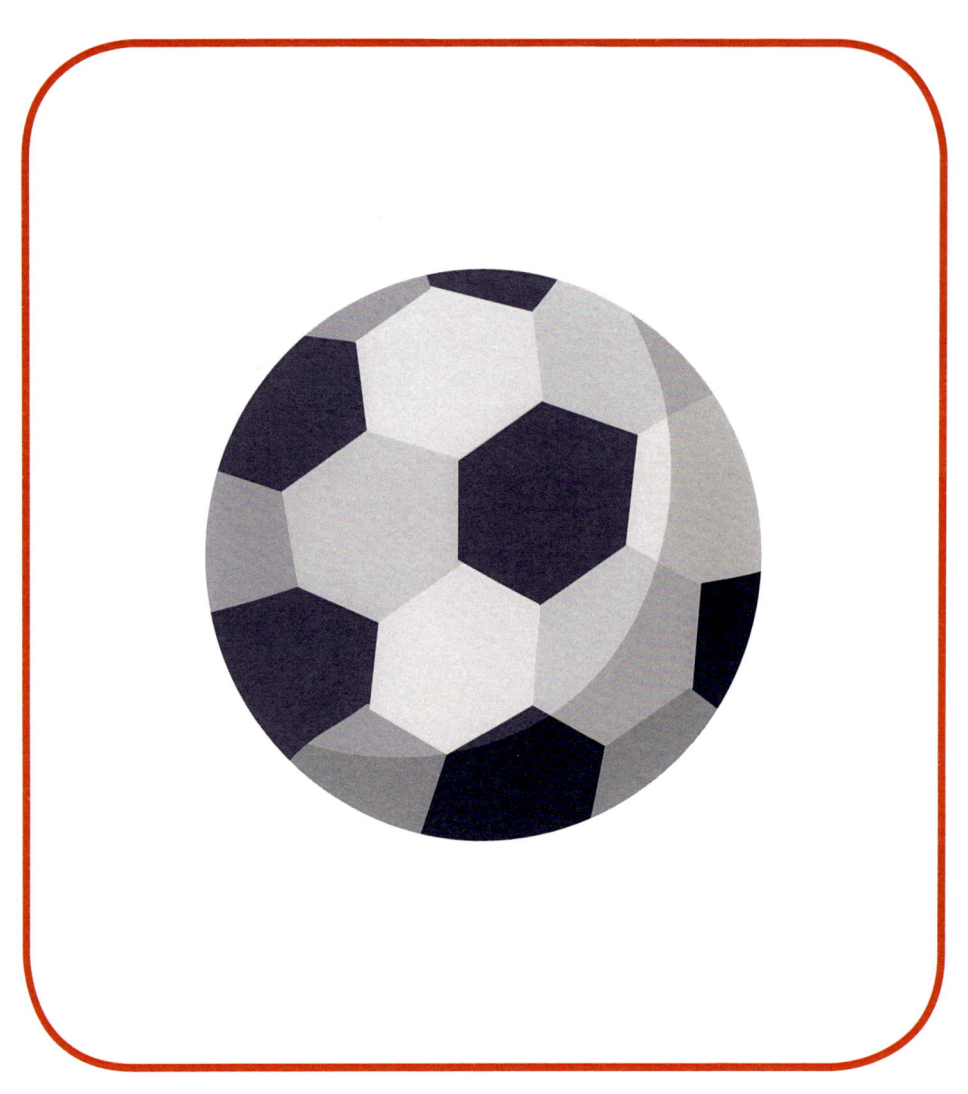

Do you have a ball?

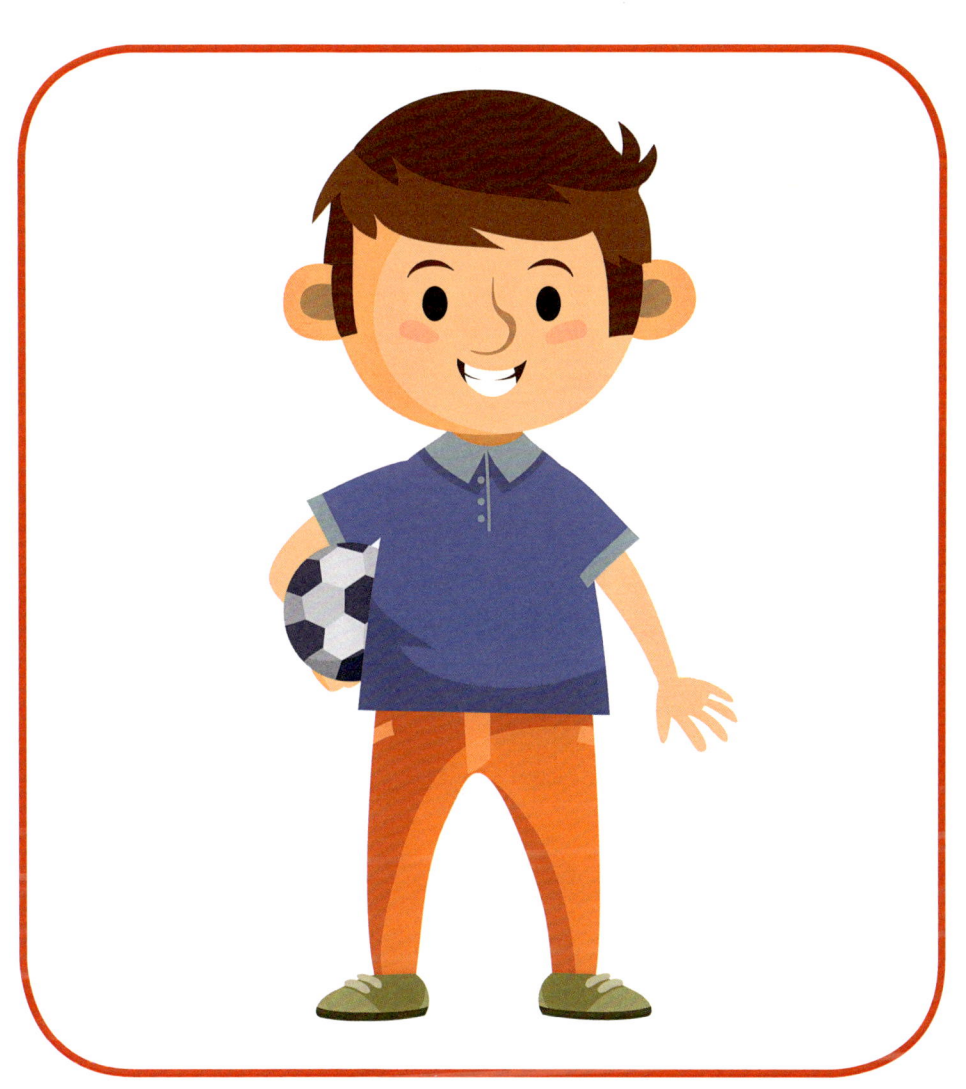

Yes, I do.

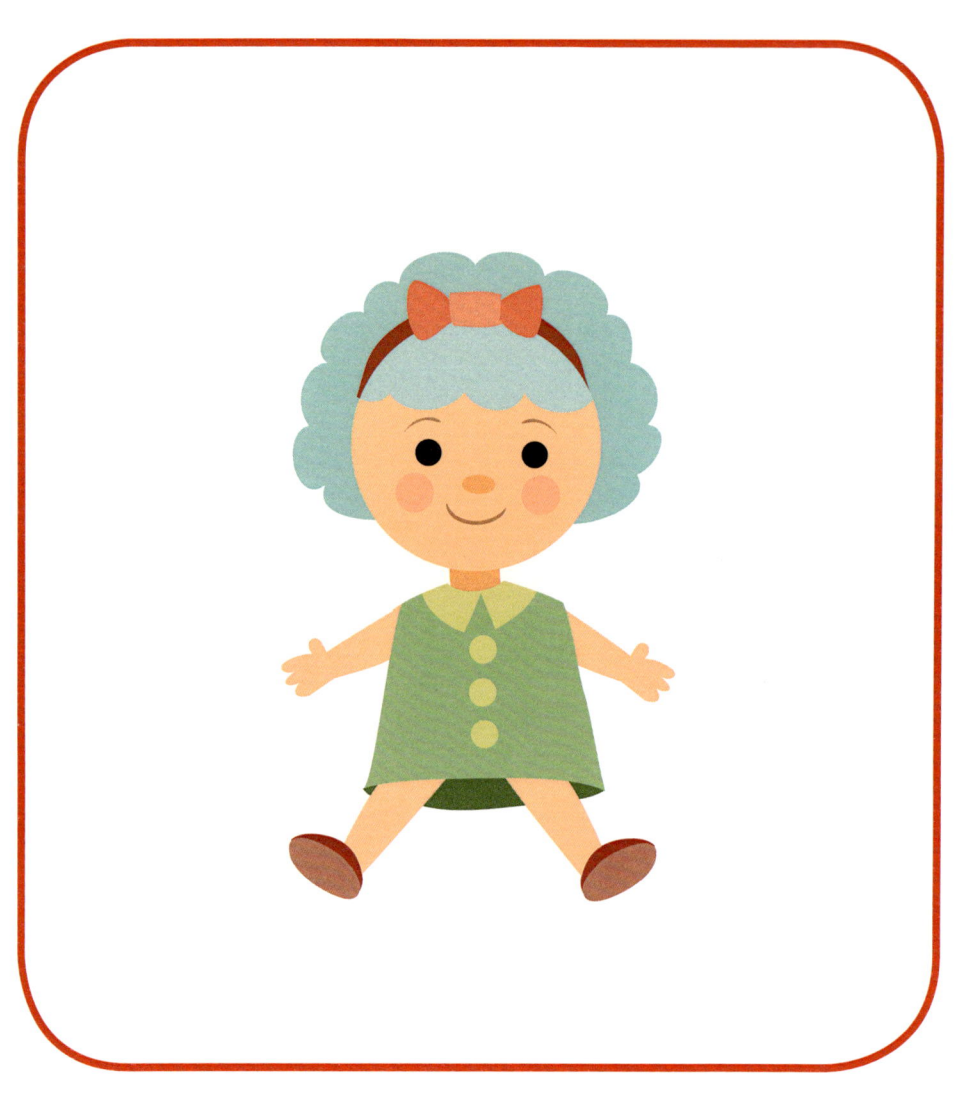

Do you have a doll?

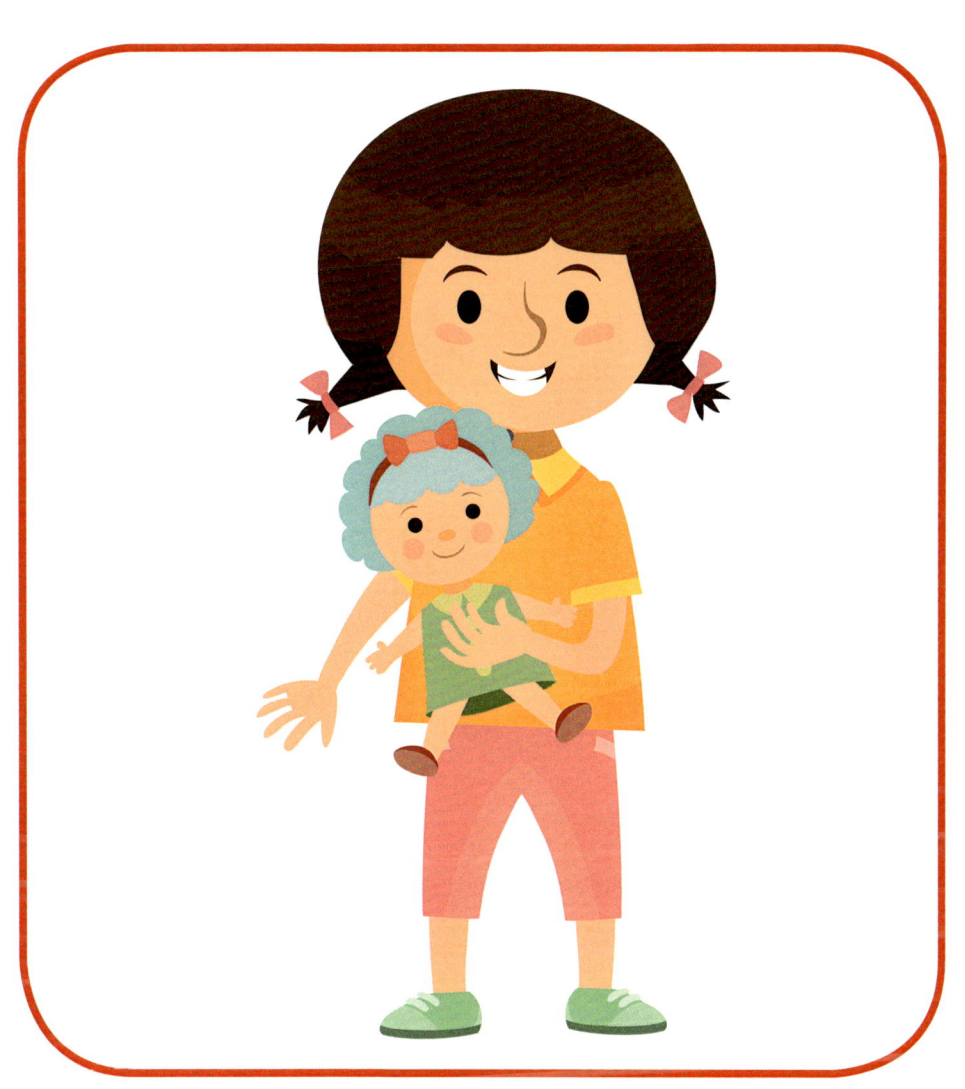

Yes, I do.

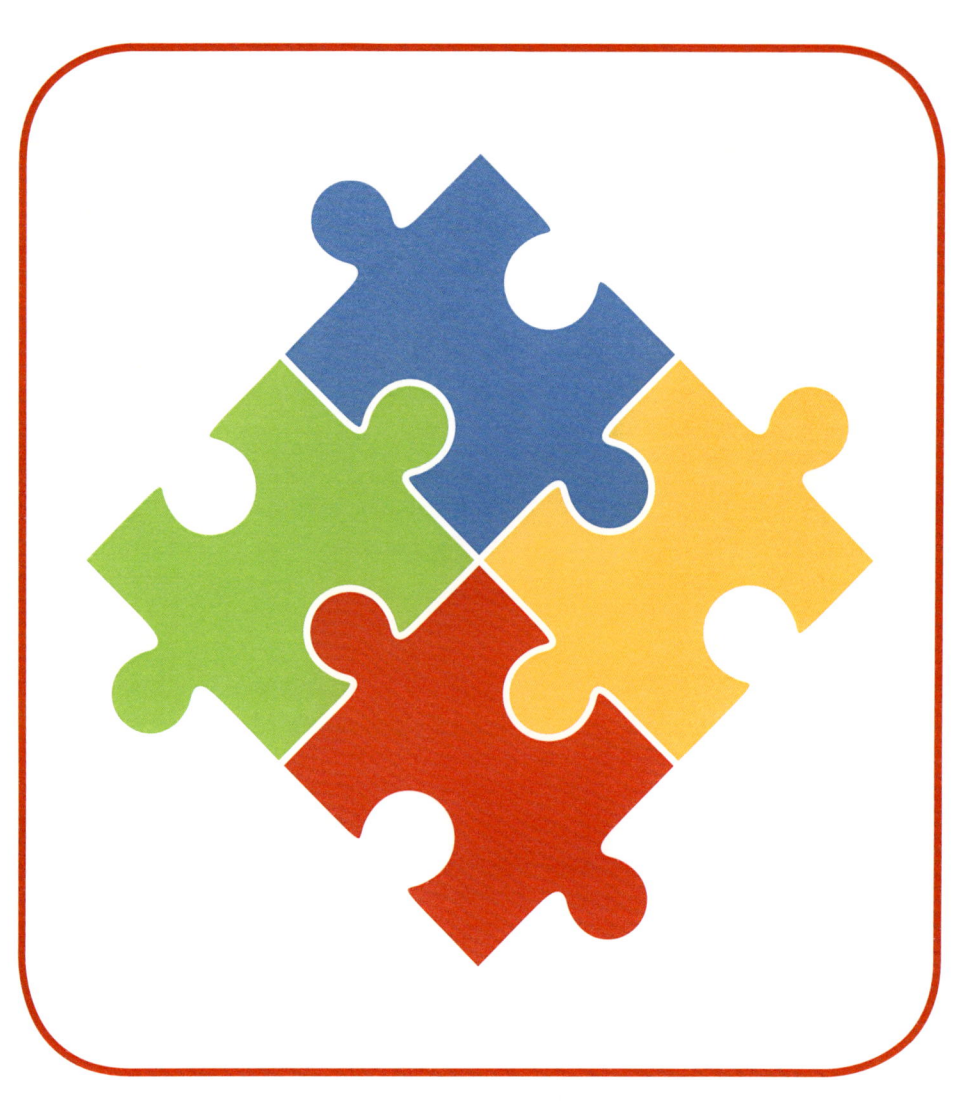

Do you have
a puzzle?

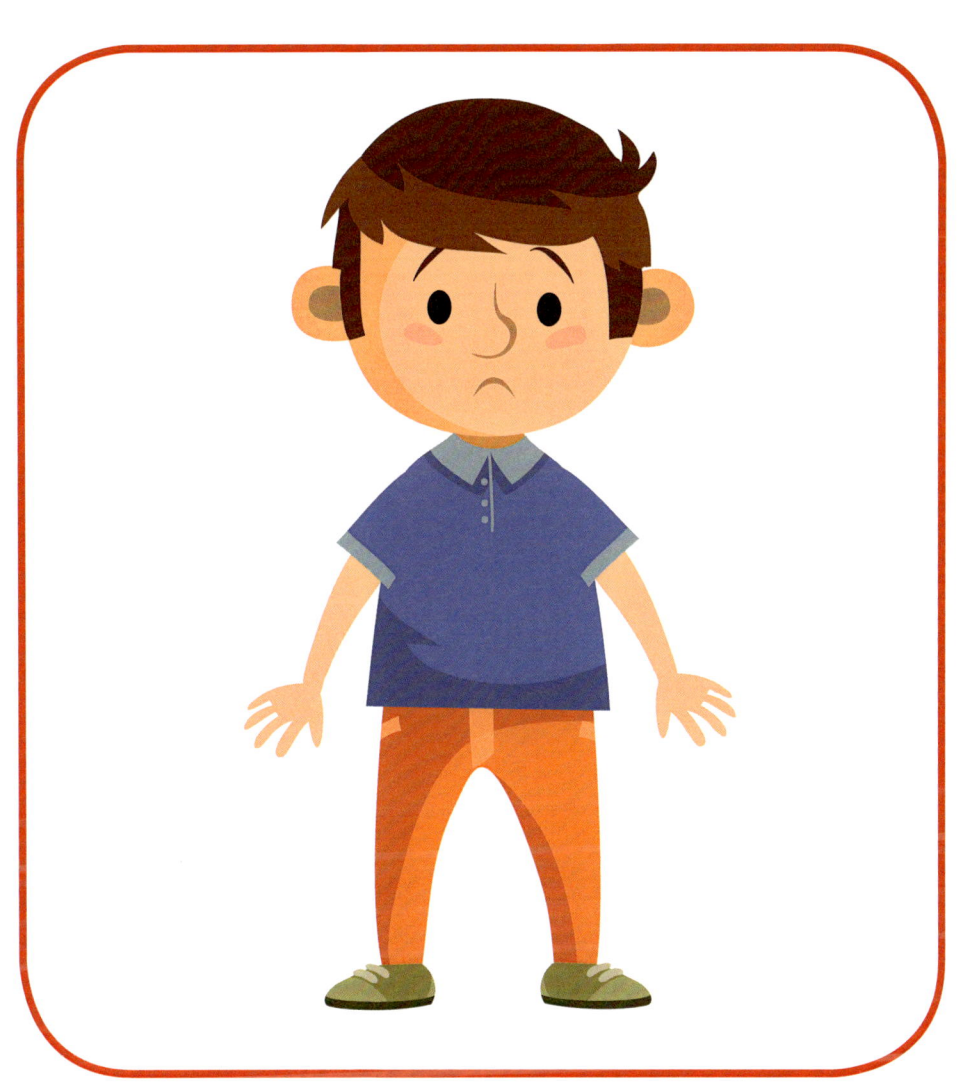

No, I don't.

Let's learn more about China.

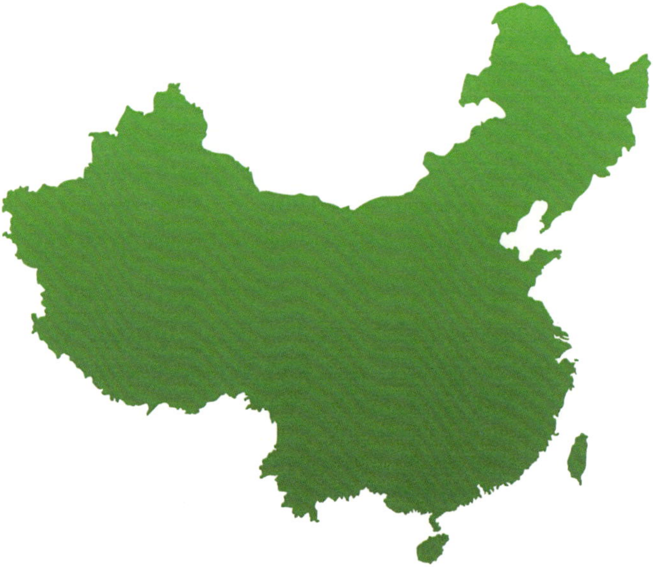

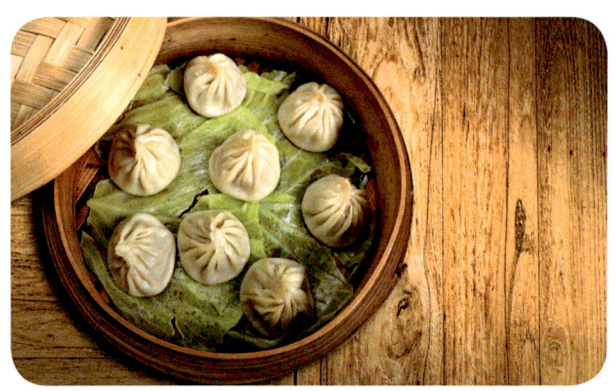

Xiaolongbao